THE ANCIENT CLIFF DWELLERS OF MESA VERDE

BY CAROLINE ARNOLD
PHOTOGRAPHS BY RICHARD HEWETT

CLARION BOOKS • NEW YORK

Photo credits: Page 48, Caroline Arnold;
pages 16–17, Mesa Verde National Park;
page 10, Gustaf Nordenskiold.
Photos on pages 22 and 39 (right) were taken with the permission
of the Southwest Museum in Los Angeles, California.
Photograph on page 10 used with the permission of the
National Board of Antiquities, Helsinki, Finland.
Map on page 3 reproduced from *The Story of Mesa Verde National Park*
by Gilbert R. Wenger. Copyright © 1980 by Mesa Verde Museum
Association, Inc., Mesa Verde National Park, Colorado 81330.

Clarion Books
a Houghton Mifflin Company imprint
215 Park Avenue South, New York, NY 10003
Text copyright © 1992 by Caroline Arnold
Photographs copyright © 1992 by Richard Hewitt

For information about permission to reproduce selections
from this book, write to Permissions, Houghton Mifflin Company,
215 Park Avenue South, New York, NY 10003.

Printed in Hong Kong.

Library of Congress Cataloging-in-Publication Data

Arnold, Caroline.
The ancient cliff dwellers of Mesa Verde / by Caroline Arnold ;
photographs by Richard Hewitt.
p.   cm.
Summary: Discusses the native Americans known as the Anasazi,
who migrated to southwestern Colorado in the first century A.D.
and mysteriously disappeared in 1300 A.D. after constructing extensive dwellings
in the cliffs of the steep canyon walls.
ISBN 0-395-56241-4   PA ISBN 0-618-05149-X
1. Pueblo Indians—History—Juvenile literature. 2. Pueblo Indians—Social life and
customs—Juvenile literature. 3. Mesa Verde National Park (Colo.)—Juvenile literature.
[1. Pueblo Indians. 2. Indians of North America—Southwest, New.
3. Cliff dwellings—Southwest, New. 4. Mesa Verde National Park (Colo.).]
I. Hewitt, Richard. II. Title
E99.P9A76   1992
978.8'27—dc20   91-8145
                              CIP
                              AC

IMS 10 9 8 7 6 5 4

ACKNOWLEDGMENTS

We are grateful to the park interpreters and staff of Mesa Verde National Park, Colorado, for their cheerful cooperation and assistance with this project. In particular we thank Robert Heyder, Park Superintendent; Donald Fiero and Linda Martin, Interpreters; and Elizabeth Bauer, Museum Curator. For their participation in the photos, we give special thanks to Cynthia Williams and Jennifer Pitt, Interpreters; Barbara Burden, Janet Marie Clausen, and the employees of Complete Archeological Services Associates in Cortez, Colorado. We also thank the Southwest Museum in Los Angeles, California, and the Museovirasto in Helsinki, Finland, for permission to photograph parts of their collections. For their expert advice, we thank Tom Weisner and Jim Hill, Department of Anthropology, University of California, Los Angeles.

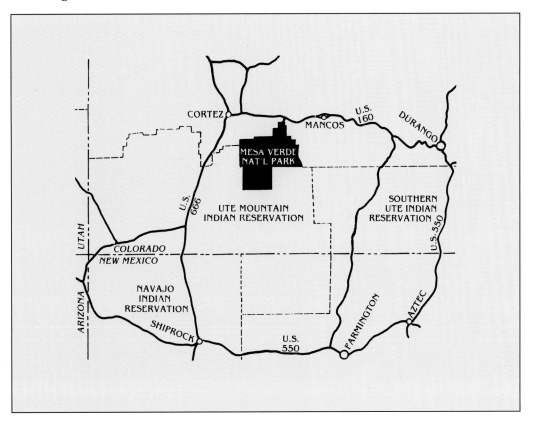

More than fourteen centuries ago, in about A.D. 550, ancient Americans came to live in southwestern Colorado in the place known today as Mesa Verde. For hundreds of years these people lived and farmed on the flat mesa top. Then, around 1190, many of them moved into alcoves in the cliffs of narrow canyons below. Nimbly climbing steep rock walls, they carried stones, water, and mud for building. Later, when the structures were complete, the inhabitants brought crops harvested from nearby fields, freshly killed wild game, and other things they needed to live. Members of the village produced pottery, baskets, and finely crafted stone and bone tools. Traders from far away came with shells, cloth, and news from the outside world. It was a thriving, productive community.

Then, in the late 1200s, less than one hundred years after they had begun building in the cliffs, the people abandoned their alcove homes in Mesa Verde, never to return. At about the same time, other groups living in the area also left their homes and moved elsewhere.

Some native Americans living in the Southwest today believe that the people who lived at Mesa Verde and nearby are their ancestors. They call them the Anasazi, a Navajo word meaning "the ancient ones."

Visitors today climb ladders similar to those used by the Anasazi.

THE DISCOVERY OF MESA VERDE

For nearly thirteen centuries, from about the year A.D. 1 to 1300, Anasazi people lived in the four corners area, so named because it is where the states of Colorado, Utah, Arizona, and New Mexico now meet. Most communities were small, but a few were clusters of many villages. One of the largest communities was at Chaco Canyon in New Mexico, which at one time housed seven thousand people.

Although each Anasazi community had its own character, they were linked by common traditions. These included a life based on the growing of corn, beans, and squash; permanent homes; similar religious customs; and the production of extremely fine pottery. The Anasazi tradition underwent many changes when the people moved, yet many of their practices are found among native Americans today.

Oak Tree House at Mesa Verde.

Vultures now soar above canyons once inhabited by the Anasazi.

Native Americans of the Ute and Navajo tribes did not move into the four corners area until about two hundred years after the Anasazi had left. The Navajo and Ute avoided going to Mesa Verde because they believed that the spirits of the ancient ones still lived there.

For hundreds of years after the Anasazi left Mesa Verde, their cliff dwellings remained virtually untouched. Roofs and walls slowly collapsed and native plants grew up in the fields the Anasazi once tilled.

In the 1770s Spanish explorers came near Mesa Verde on their way west, and they saw the steep slopes of the high plateau that rises sharply above the plain. They probably gave it the name Mesa Verde, which means "green table" in Spanish, but they never went onto the mesa or ventured into its canyons.

Cliff Palace.

In the 1880s, conflict between the native Americans and the United States government had forced most native Americans to live on reservations. In southwestern Colorado, ranchers and miners of European descent were settling nonreservation land. They discovered numerous small cliff dwellings in the area around Mesa Verde. But, although there were stories of more cliff dwellings on Mesa Verde, that land was part of the Ute Mountain Indian Reservation and few outsiders had seen them.

The Wetherills, a family of ranchers living in Mancos, Colorado, became friendly with the Ute and obtained permission from them to graze their cattle in Mesa Verde during the winter

months. On December 18, 1888, Richard Wetherill and his brother-in-law, Charles Mason, were riding across the mesa in search of lost cattle. They came to the edge of a steep canyon, and when they looked across for their missing animals, they saw instead a complex of abandoned stone buildings wedged under the overhanging rock of the canyon wall. Some of the structures towered four stories high; others surrounded large, round pits; and in many there were remnants of pottery, baskets, and other signs that people had once lived there. The two cowboys had discovered Cliff Palace, a village that had once housed more than two hundred people. It is the largest cliff ruin in Mesa Verde.

Photo by Gustaf Nordenskiold of Balcony House, 1891.

Over the next few years the Wetherills continued to explore in Mesa Verde, and they discovered and named other ruins. When news of the cliff dwellings was made public, many other people came to see them. The visitors were interested in finding out how people had lived before the first Europeans came to America. They also came to collect pottery and other souvenirs.

The first systematic investigation of Mesa Verde was conducted in 1891 by a Swede named Gustaf Nordenskiold. He had originally come to America hoping that the dry climate of the Southwest would cure his tuberculosis. When he heard about the cliff houses at Mesa Verde he became intrigued and made arrangements to visit them. Nordenskiold wrote detailed descriptions of what he found at Mesa Verde and later published them in a book. He also took photographs that provide us with important information about the condition of the ruins at that time.

Like the Wetherills and many other visitors to the Mesa Verde ruins, Nordenskiold began his own collection of pottery, tools, and other items found in the abandoned village. When he prepared to ship his finds to Sweden, many people were upset that items of such obvious historical value should be allowed to leave the country, but at that time there were no laws to prevent it. The Nordenskiold collection is now exhibited in the National Museum of Helsinki, Finland.

Black and white geometric designs are typical of Anasazi pottery.

After the Mesa Verde ruins were discovered, many people felt that the United States government should find a way to protect the dwellings and the objects inside them. A Colorado woman named Virginia McClurg began a campaign on behalf of Mesa Verde. She lectured widely to gain support for the cause and organized the Mesa Verde Cliff Dwellers Association. She also helped make an arrangement with the Ute that allowed the ruins to be protected but gave the Ute people the right to graze their animals in the park. Finally, on June 2, 1906, President Theodore Roosevelt signed the bill that made Mesa Verde into a national park. Mesa Verde is the only national park in the United States established to preserve the works of prehistoric people.

Every year thousands of people from all over the world come to Mesa Verde National Park. They learn about the Anasazi by talking with park rangers, viewing the ruins, and visiting the park museum. On the mesa top visitors can explore numerous ruins and excavations; dozens of other ruins can be viewed from cliff top overlooks. During the summer months five cliff dwellings can be visited. Self-guided tours can be made to Cliff Palace, Spruce Tree House, and Step House. Park rangers lead tours to Long House and Balcony House. Spruce Tree House is the only cliff dwelling open to the public during the winter.

Visitors view a kiva at Balcony House.
"Kiva" is a Hopi word for a ceremonial room.

UNCOVERING THE PAST

During the years that Mesa Verde has been a park, it has been the site of many excavation projects, both of the cliff dwellings and of the mesa top ruins. Early excavations were done by Dr. Jesse Walter Fewkes, who worked in the park for the Smithsonian Institution. Under his supervision many tools and other objects were recovered and some of the ruins were repaired. Dr. Fewkes started the first park museum in 1917.

In recent years survey teams have crisscrossed the Mesa Verde park terrain to locate additional sites of archeological importance. These have been mapped, and some have been excavated. They include the remains of buildings, fire pits, and farming and irrigation projects. Nearly four thousand sites have been found, including the remains of more than six hundred cliff dwellings.

When an object is found it is numbered and identified, and its location at the site is noted. It is then brought to the Mesa Verde Research Center where it is cleaned, catalogued, and stored in a large metal cabinet. The collection is available for study by both park staff and outside researchers who have made arrangements with the park superintendent.

The kinds of things that a group of people do as well as their clothes, food, dwellings, and beliefs form their culture. We can find out about past cultures by examining the objects people have left behind and by noting changes that people have made to their environment. Archeologists are scientists who dig up, identify, and sometimes remove such evidence of earlier cultures.

Left, above: Sorting pottery pieces for storage.
Left, below: Stone axe heads were either held by hand or lashed onto wooden handles.

Archeology is part of the much larger field of anthropology, the study of humankind. Anthropologists try to find out why people live as they do by studying their cultures. By comparing different cultures, both in the past and in the present, anthropologists learn what makes each one unique.

We will never know everything about how an ancient people such as the Anasazi lived, but the combined efforts of many experts help make the picture more complete. For instance, medical experts examine human remains and help us to understand what kinds of diseases the Anasazi may have had. Botanists and zoologists study the plant and animal life of the time. Geologists study the land and climatologists learn about the weather. All of this information gives us insight into what life may have been like for the Anasazi.

Pottery discovered on Wetherill Mesa at Mesa Verde.

When studying a culture such as that of the Anasazi, it is important to know how old an ancient building or object might be. One method of dating objects, called stratigraphy, is the study of the layers in which objects are deposited in the ground. At Mesa Verde and elsewhere, living sites were often used over many years, with newer houses built on top of the places where old houses had been. Also, as we do in modern times, the Anasazi communities usually dumped their trash in one place. Over the years their refuse collected in large heaps, with the oldest trash buried on the bottom and the newest on top. Thus, as archeologists dig down at living sites or trash heaps, they find older and older material. Sometimes two different sites contain objects of similar styles, and this indicates that the two sites are of similar age. This is called cross-dating.

Some of the most commonly found objects at Mesa Verde and at other Anasazi sites are pottery, or pieces of broken pottery which are called shards. Techniques of pottery making changed both over time and by location. Experts can usually tell a pot's age and where it was made by its construction and decoration.

In Mesa Verde, the dating of the ruins is usually done by looking at sections of wooden beams in the buildings. As a tree grows, it produces rings—a light ring in spring and a dark ring in summer. Because the rings are wide in wet seasons and narrow in dry seasons, they reveal the pattern of weather during a tree's life. All trees growing in the same area develop a similar pattern. Thus, by comparing the growth rings on a house beam with those of a tree of known age, scientists can figure out the date that the tree was cut down. This system of tree-ring dating is called dendrochronology.

Another technique that is sometimes used to date archeological finds is called palynology, the study of plant pollen. Every flowering plant produces its own kind of pollen. By looking through a microscope at preserved specimens, experts can identify what kinds of plants the Anasazi were growing as crops, as well as what kinds of native plants grew in the area.

Upper left: Crosscut log reveals weathered growth rings.
Upper right: Wild sunflowers are common at Mesa Verde.
Below: Pottery shards.

HISTORY OF THE ANASAZI

It is thought that the first people came to North and South America about thirty thousand years ago by walking across an ice and land bridge between Asia and Alaska. Gradually moving south, they dispersed across the two continents. Although people did not live at Mesa Verde until much later, remains of campsites and stone spear points indicate that people were living in the four corners area as early as ten thousand years ago. These people gathered wild plants and hunted large animals such as deer and bison.

Mule deer.

The atlatl helped a hunter to hurl his spear harder and farther than he could by holding the spear with his hand.

These early Americans lived simple, nomadic lives for thousands of years. Then, about the year A.D. 1, they learned how to grow corn and squash from their neighbors to the south. Now their way of life changed from one in which they were constantly on the move in search of food to a more settled existence that depended more on the crops they grew themselves. Like their ancestors, they continued to hunt wild game, using throwing devices called atlatls as weapons.

Communities were formed by small family groups living in shallow rock alcoves. Because its people produced very fine baskets, this new culture was given the name Basket Maker by archeologists. Baskets were used to carry and store food and other items.

A basket could be made waterproof with a coating of sticky pine pitch. One way the Basket Makers cooked was by dropping fire-heated stones into a basket containing food and water. The hot stones made the water boil, which then cooked the food. It was not an ideal way to prepare food because cooking was slow and often uneven.

The Basket Maker culture existed from about A.D. 1 to 550 and is considered the first period of Anasazi culture. Although the early Basket Makers did not live at Mesa Verde, they are the ancestors of the first people who did.

Left: Corn and squash plants. Right: Basket.

About A.D. 550 some of the Basket Maker people moved to Mesa Verde. Numerous changes occurred in Anasazi life at this time, so archeologists call the interval from A.D. 550 to 750 the Modified Basket Maker period. The Anasazi began to build their first permanent dwellings, which were called pithouses because the floors were formed by digging shallow pits into the ground. A hole in the roof of the pithouse was both an entrance and a place for smoke to escape. Some pithouses also had a second small chamber, which was used for storage. The remains of several pithouses are often found together, indicating that families preferred to live in small villages.

Another important change that occurred during this period was that the Basket Makers learned to make pottery. Clay pots greatly improved the way food was stored and cooked. They were strong and made good, animalproof storage containers. And unlike baskets, which would burn when placed in fire, pots could be placed directly on the flames. Thus food could be cooked much more thoroughly than before.

The high elevation of Mesa Verde, which is about seven thousand feet above sea level, makes it slightly cooler in summer and wetter than the plain below. Both the climate and rich soil made it a good place to grow crops. Beans were added to the Anasazi diet during this period, and were an important source of protein. Anasazi beans were very much like today's pinto beans. The Anasazi ate them fresh and also dried them to be used later.

Left above: Cutaway view of a reconstructed pithouse shows the poles used for support and fire ring inside.
Left below: Beans were often collected on vines and then picked.

In about A.D. 750, the Anasazi's way of life began to change again. Now, instead of building pithouses, they constructed square rooms with vertical walls. Often these rooms were joined together in a line or semicircle to form a small community. Archeologists call this kind of architecture "pueblo," from the Spanish word meaning "village." For the Anasazi at Mesa Verde, the time between A.D. 750 and 1100 is called the Developmental Pueblo period.

The pueblos at Mesa Verde were usually built on the mesa top. The men of the village cleared small fields close by and dug the ground with long wooden sticks to prepare it for planting. When

The Anasazi used the roofs of their house

the crops were ripe, everyone helped with the harvest. Much of the food was dried and stored so that it could be used during the winter or in years when the crops failed due to bad weather.

The first pueblo houses were built with wooden posts and walls of sun-dried mud. Sometimes the houses had a row of stones around the base; later the Anasazi built entire walls of stone, which made the houses sturdier and more permanent.

In front of the pueblo, there was often a single room dug into the ground. This was used as a social gathering place for religious ceremonies. As time went on, these rooms, which are called kivas, became a more important part of Anasazi life.

or working and as places to dry foods.

Pots in the black and white style.

Natural deposits of clay are found throughout the Mesa Verde area and are easy to dig out of the ground. Anasazi pots were made by the women of the community, and each potter developed her own variations of traditional designs. Finished pots were hardened by baking them in a small bonfire.

During the Developmental Pueblo period, the Anasazi began making two types of pottery, one for eating and the other for cooking. All pots were made by coiling narrow strips of clay in a circular pattern, and pinching them together to build a wall. For cups, ladles, bowls, and other eating utensils and vessels, the coils were usually smoothed out to make a flat surface. They were then coated with a light-colored clay and painted with a black or brown stain made from berry juices or crushed minerals. The usual designs were intricate patterns of lines, squares, and other geometric shapes.

Cooking pots and water vessels did not have painted designs. Instead, the potter left her pinch marks in the clay, creating a coarse, patterned surface. These indentations are called corrugations; in some cases they actually reveal the fingerprints of the maker. The rough surfaces of these pots made them less slippery and easier to handle. The greater surface area also helped the pot heat better when it was used for cooking.

In addition to eating and cooking containers, clay was also used to make small figurines, which were probably used for religious purposes, and to make pipes for smoking wild tobacco.

Pot in the corrugated style.

Far View House ruin.

Around A.D. 1100, many of the small villages across the mesa began to merge into fewer, larger communities. This final period of Anasazi culture, which lasted until about 1300, is known as the Classic, or Great, Pueblo period. At the height of its development, the entire Mesa Verde population may have numbered three to five thousand people. Some villages, such as those at Far View, became large, multiroomed complexes with sleeping, storage, and social rooms all joined together. The largest structure at Far View, called Far View House, once contained fifty rooms and five kivas, and was two stories high. The remains of numerous other smaller villages are only a short walk from Far View House.

Small dams and what may have been a large reservoir show that people of the Far View community must have worked together to make sure that their crops would grow and that they would have enough food to eat.

Water was an essential resource for the people at Mesa Verde. For many years rangers at Mesa Verde National Park planted a small plot of corn as an experiment. Just as the Anasazi had done long ago, they relied on summer rains to water their crop. Except for three very dry years, the corn grew well in more than fifty other seasons.

On average, there are only eighteen inches of rain each year, just enough to grow crops such as corn or beans successfully. The only other sources of water are a few small springs along the canyon walls, plus runoff water from storms or melting snow.

Spring near Spruce Tree House.

Above: Cedar Tree Tower is one of fifty-seven round towers found at Mesa Verde. Right: The spiral pattern in this stone may have been used as a kind of solar calendar.

The Anasazi people were peaceful, but it is possible that during hard times they quarreled among themselves. During the last period at Mesa Verde, the Anasazi began to build towers, which may have been used to send signals or to watch for approaching visitors. Other explanations for the towers are that they may have had a religious purpose or may have been used to chart the sun and keep track of the seasons. For a community that depended on a successful harvest for its food supply, it was important to know when to plant each crop for best results.

Between A.D. 1150 and 1200, the Mesa Verde people moved again, this time into large, shallow alcoves along the canyon walls. Although these ledges and alcoves had been used for hundreds of years for sleeping and shelter, now the Anasazi began to build villages there. They built their houses into the natural contours of the canyon walls and tucked rooms into almost every available space. Because the cliff overhangs protected these villages from the worst effects of wind and weather, many are remark-

Cliff Palace.

Although some Anasazi remained on the mesa top, the majority moved into the new alcove villages. One wonders why so many people were willing to abandon their mesa top homes for cliff dwellings that were, by comparison, dark, damp, and farther from their sources of food. On the one hand, the cliff ledges offered some protection from the weather. Some are built on south-facing walls so that they stay cool during the day but take advantage of the heat of the afternoon sun. This is particularly true in the winter when the sun is low in the sky.

People who lived in the cliff dwellings would have had to make daily trips to the mesa top to tend their fields. At Step House, you can see the remains of a stone staircase that the Anasazi built up the side of the cliff. More often, however, they ascended the cliff by following a series of hand and toe holds carved into the rock. Within the cliff dwellings, the Anasazi used ladders to get from one level to another.

Some of the cliff dwellings are built onto ledges that seem impossible to approach from any direction. It has been suggested that the Anasazi moved into cliff houses because they were easier to defend in the case of an attack. On the other hand, cliff dwellers risked being trapped if attackers cut off their routes of escape. We do not know of any other groups living in the four corners area before A.D. 1400, so it is unlikely the Anasazi would have been attacked by outsiders. Decapitated skeletons and other evidence of violence in the four corners region (though not at Mesa Verde), does indicate that the Anasazi did sometimes quarrel among themselves.

Far left: House of Many Windows.
Left above: Ladder.
Left below: Toe holds.

In the dry climate of the Southwest, corn could be preserved for a long time. A small bowl covering the top of this jar protected the corn inside for more than seven hundred years.

DAILY LIFE

The most important food crop for the Anasazi was corn. Corn was originally developed as a crop in central Mexico and was brought to the North American region from there. Although there is evidence of corn in the Southwest from as long as 5,600 years ago, corn was not grown as a major crop in the four corners area until the Anasazi period. The corn that the Anasazi grew was a hard, multicolored type with black, red, and yellow kernels.

Women were responsible for preparing and cooking food. They ground the corn, crushing it with a hand-held stone called a mano against a flat stone slab called a metate. As part of this process grit from the stone became mixed with the cornmeal. Over time, the grit in the food wore down the teeth of the Anasazi.

Although we cannot know exactly how the Anasazi prepared all of their foods, we can guess how they might have done so by studying the cooking and eating customs of modern pueblo cultures. They probably used the coarse cornmeal to make a flat bread, which was then baked in the ashes of the fire or on top of a thin stone griddle. Cornmeal could also be made into dumpling-like balls and boiled in soups or stews. Other vegetables such as beans and squash were cooked alone or with meat. Foods were flavored with salt or with wild plants such as mustard or onion.

While women worked, their babies were tucked snugly into cradle boards which the women wore on their backs or propped nearby. Older children played or helped with simple tasks.

Left: Manos and metates are among the most commonly found objects at Mesa Verde. Right: Cradle board.

Left: A bee gathers nectar to make honey. Right: Piñon pine and cone.

In addition to the foods they grew, the Anasazi also harvested edible wild plants. They ate roots, berries, nuts, greens, cacti, seeds, and fruits. Wild honey was also available as a natural sweetener.

A wild food still eaten today is the prickly pear cactus. Its red fruit is sweet and good raw or cooked. The spines are removed either by rolling the fruit against a hard surface or by burning them off. The Anasazi probably ate the fleshy green stems of the prickly pear either raw, roasted, stewed, or dried and ground into meal.

Berries of the Utah juniper were used to flavor foods and also dried to make jewelry. The whole juniper tree was valuable to the Anasazi. Its shaggy bark was used for roofs, stuffed into sandals to

Left: The Utah juniper. Right: Prickly pear cactus.

make them warm in winter, and even sometimes used inside pillows. The wood of the tree was used to make bows and for fuel.

The other most common tree at Mesa Verde is the piñon pine. Like most plants that grow on the mesa top, it is well adapted to a semiarid climate. The Anasazi ate piñon nuts, from the cone of the tree, either raw or ground into a paste. The sticky sap, or gum, of the piñon tree was used to mend cracks in pottery and to waterproof baskets used for cooking and storage of food. In some pueblo cultures today, when a person dies, piñon gum is burned and the family members inhale the smoke as protection against evil spirits. The Anasazi may have done this too. Piñon needles were used as medicine, and the wood was used in building houses and for fuel.

The broadleaf yucca was among the most useful of all the native plants. In early summer the yucca produces a tall, white flower which later develops into large, green fruits somewhat resembling fat cucumbers. These can be peeled and eaten raw or cooked. The roots of the plant can be used like soap and give yucca its common name, soapweed. The long, spiked leaves of yucca contain strong fibers. These are obtained by boiling the leaves to soften them so that the outer covering can be removed. The fibers are then twisted into cords. The Anasazi used yucca cords to make a wide variety of articles including sandals, ropes, animal snares, and baskets.

Far left: Broadleaf yucca. Below left: The longest yucca cord found at Mesa Verde was over 1,300 feet long. Below right: Yucca-fiber sandals protected the feet from rocks, heat, and sharp-spined cactus.

Only 212 buried skeletons have been found among the Mesa Verde ruins, which is not very many considering that so many people lived there. They indicate that Anasazi men were an average height of about five feet four inches tall and that women were slightly shorter. Few people lived longer than forty years and when living conditions worsened, they died at even younger ages. Older people and babies were especially susceptible during the cold winter months. We don't know exactly what diseases they died of, but examinations of their bones show that many older people suffered from arthritis. Their teeth, though worn down by the grit in their diet, show that the Anasazi had fewer cavities than most Americans today.

Archeologists have found a large number of turkey droppings near Anasazi dwellings. Until recently, wild turkeys were common at Mesa Verde, and in Anasazi times they were apparently kept as domestic animals. Dogs were also kept as pets.

Merriam's Turkey.

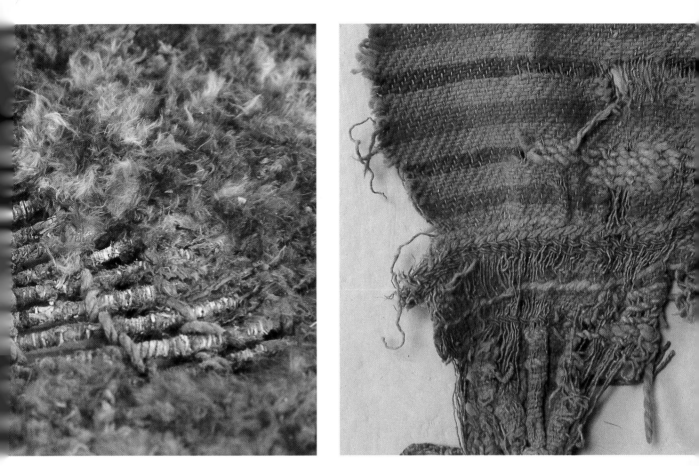

Left: Turkey-feather blanket. Right: Cotton cloth.

The Anasazi used turkey feathers to make warm blankets or robes. Winter temperatures at Mesa Verde are often below freezing, and these blankets would have been a good way to keep warm. Animal skins also provided covering in cold weather.

As in most of the Southwest, summer weather in Mesa Verde is hot and dry, and probably the Anasazi wore little clothing in summer. Only a few pieces of Anasazi clothing have been found and not much is known about how they were worn. Apparently men wore loincloths, while women wore small aprons. Although pieces of cotton cloth have been found at Mesa Verde, experiments have shown that cotton plants cannot grow to maturity in the Mesa Verde climate. Cotton must have been traded with people who lived farther south.

About A.D. 700–750, during the Modified Basket Maker period, bows and arrows had replaced the atlatl as the preferred hunting weapon. The bow and arrow was more accurate, had a longer range, and could be fired more rapidly. The atlatl required the hunter to stand up in order to have the full sweep of his arm for throwing, whereas a bow hunter could hide in ambush for game.

Bows were made of a single piece of wood with a bowstring of sinew or yucca rope. Wooden arrows were tipped with either sharpened wood points or stone points carved from local rocks such as quartz, flint, and obsidian.

Many kinds of animals lived on the mesa top and in the canyons below. Sources of meat included mule deer, which are still common, as well as rock squirrels, cottontails and jack rabbits, dusky grouse, and wood rats.

The straight branches of the cliff fendler bush made good arrows.

Carved stone arrowheads.

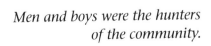

Men and boys were the hunters
of the community.

The men of each community were usually responsible for building houses and other structures. Using stone axes, they cut logs for floor and roof supports and chipped pieces of sandstone into rectangular building blocks. Sandstone is found throughout the Mesa Verde area, frequently breaking off into rough blocks. Expert craftsmen then shaped the soft sandstone into square-edged building stones.

A thin layer of mud was usually plastered over house walls to make them smooth. Sometimes this plaster was decorated with a contrasting color. Except on a few well-protected walls, these plaster coatings have been washed off by centuries of weather.

In front of the rooms where people lived, the Anasazi constructed underground kivas where people met for community meetings and religious ceremonies. Probably the Anasazi used the kivas to conduct healing rites, or to pray for rain, for good luck in hunting, or for good crops. The Anasazi also used the kivas for weaving.

Below: The missing floor allows the plaster decorations in this second story room to be seen from underneath. Far right: Diorama showing the construction of a kiva.

Above: Tunnel entrance to a kiva. Far right: The only light in a kiva came from the fire or the hole in the roof.

A typical kiva of the Great Pueblo period was round, with six stone roof supports resting on a narrow shelf. In the center was a fire pit, a short wall to deflect the fire's heat, and a small hole in the floor called a sipapu. According to present-day pueblo cultures, the sipapu represents an entrance to the underworld of the spirits.

When the kiva was finished, the roof was covered except for the hole for a ladder. Sometimes the kiva could also be entered through a small tunnel in one of the walls. Such tunnels may have served as ventilator holes. Pueblo cultures today use them to create special effects. For instance, a person can hide in the tunnel and then pop out suddenly at a dramatic point in the ceremony.

Religion was part of everyday experience and influenced all aspects of Anasazi life. Kivas are found in almost every Anasazi community and are a distinguishing feature of the culture. In some places the Anasazi also built huge ceremonial rooms called great kivas where several families could meet.

The top of the kiva, which was at ground level, formed a small courtyard. It was in such areas that most village life took place. In the open space food was prepared; tools, pots, and baskets were made; children played; and people met to talk and relax. Probably, except when it was very cold, rooms inside buildings were used mainly for sleeping or storage. In winter, thin stone slabs were placed over door and window openings as protection against the weather.

T-shaped doors are found in many cliff dwellings. Such doorways were less drafty, and the larger opening on top allowed a person carrying a load to enter more easily. It may be that the T shape also had religious or cultural significance.

Upper stories of buildings were entered from stairways or ladders inside a lower room, from neighboring rooftops, or from ladders up to narrow outside balconies. Although these balconies have now crumbled, the support beams are visible in many of the ruins.

Courtyard at Spruce Tree House.

One of the most unusual structures at Mesa Verde is the Sun Temple, built on top of the mesa on a point of land opposite Cliff Palace. Shaped like an enormous D, it probably was intended for a religious or ceremonial purpose. Yet this ambitious structure was never finished. Work stopped in the late 1200s when many of the Anasazi were leaving Mesa Verde.

Between A.D. 1250 and 1300 the Anasazi abandoned their homes in Mesa Verde and traveled south. It is believed that some Anasazi settled along the Rio Grande River in northern New Mexico and that others joined the Hopi and Zuñi peoples of Arizona and western New Mexico. As the Anasazi merged with other groups, they forgot many of their old ways and adopted new customs. Some of the present-day native Americans in the Southwest are probably descendants of the Anasazi, but it is difficult to tell which of their traditions are from the Anasazi and which are adapted from other cultures.

In modern times the space between the double walls of the Sun Temple was covered with cement to seal the inside from dampness.

WHY DID THE ANASAZI LEAVE MESA VERDE?

By the thirteenth century, the Mesa Verde population had grown to several thousand people. Every bit of suitable land was being used for crops, and constant use had depleted many of its valuable nutrients. As more land became cleared to grow crops, hunters had to search farther for wild game. It was also becoming harder to find enough wood for building and for fuel.

Throughout Anasazi life at Mesa Verde there had been periodic droughts. Usually a drought lasted for just a few growing seasons. But in 1276, a disastrous pattern of weather began.

Year after year crops failed because there was not enough rain in summer or snow in winter. Unusually cool weather shortened the growing season as well. People could not live without food, so one by one, family groups began to move away. In some cases, they left behind clothing, tools, and small supplies of food, as if they intended to return. By the time the drought was over twenty-three years later, everyone had left Mesa Verde. Perhaps the Anasazi intended to come back to their homes in Mesa Verde. Yet in the centuries that followed, no one ever did.

Long House.

For many years scientists have debated why the Anasazi left Mesa Verde. Some people have suggested that they were driven out by warfare, and it does appear that more conflicts broke out when times were bad. Yet there is no evidence so far that there was conflict on a massive scale. Other people have suggested that the Anasazi died in an epidemic, but again the lack of mass graves suggests that this was not the case.

We know that the Anasazi had survived worse droughts earlier in their history. The lack of rain would have made life difficult, but even at the peak of the drought in the late 1200s, Anasazi were constructing new communities elsewhere in the region. Recently, scientists have gathered evidence from various Anasazi sites in the Southwest showing that the pattern of building a community and then abandoning it after a few generations was not unusual. Unlike some other ancient civilizations, such as those of Greece and Rome, in which cities had a more or less continuous development over hundreds or thousands of years, the Anasazi culture was one in which people built communities and then moved on. Nevertheless, most experts believe that it was the drought, combined with other factors, that was the greatest influence on the Anasazi's move away from the four corners region.

This large rock carving, or petroglyph, is found at Petroglyph Point in Mesa Verde. According to an interpretation by modern Hopis, it represents various Anasazi clans and their journeys. The work is signed with the artist's hand.

During the eight centuries that the Anasazi culture existed at Mesa Verde, it changed from a relatively simple farming life to a society organized into developed villages. The problems that probably forced the Anasazi to leave Mesa Verde and the surrounding area—a growing population, the depletion of natural resources, a change in the climate, possible internal conflict—are the same issues that we face today on a global level. The plight of the Anasazi illustrates how important it is to use one's resources wisely and how a slight shift in climate can change a good life to a marginal existence.

What is so amazing about visiting Mesa Verde is how much there is to see and how well everything has been preserved. The dwellings and objects left behind give us a glimpse into the past and the chance to see what life might have been like on that fertile tableland many centuries ago. Mesa Verde is the largest archeological preserve in the United States, containing more cliff dwellings than have been found anywhere else. That the Anasazi accomplished all this peacefully, and by using only stone tools, is incredible indeed.

Far View House at sunset.

GLOSSARY

Anasazi—a native American culture of the Southwest that began about A.D. 1 and existed until A.D. 1300 or longer.

anthropology—the study of humankind.

archeology—the study of any prehistoric culture by excavation and description of its remains.

arthritis—a disease in which the joints are inflamed.

atlatl—a spear-throwing device used by ancient peoples such as the Anasazi.

Basket Maker period—the span of Anasazi culture from A.D. 1–550.

botany—the study of plants.

Classic Pueblo period—the span of Anasazi culture from A.D. 1100–1300; also called the Great Pueblo period.

climatology—the study of climates.

corrugations—the pattern of surface indentations found on Anasazi cookware.

cross-dating—the dating of archeological sites by comparing similar objects from different locations.

culture—a people's activities as well as their clothes, food, dwellings, and beliefs.

dendrochronology—the dating of wooden objects by comparing the tree rings with samples of known age.

Developmental Pueblo period—the span of Anasazi culture from A.D. 750–1100.

Fewkes, Dr. Jesse Walter—a scientist who did excavations at Mesa Verde for the Smithsonian Institution.

geology—the study of the earth and the rocks of which it is composed.

Hopi—a present-day pueblo culture in Arizona and New Mexico.

kiva—a Hopi word for a ceremonial room.

mano—a hand-held stone used for crushing corn.

Mason, Charles—one of two cowboys credited with the discovery of Mesa Verde.

McClurg, Virginia—a Colorado citizen who campaigned to make Mesa Verde into a national park.

mesa—a landform having a relatively flat top and bounded by steep rock walls.

Mesa Verde—a national park in the southwestern corner of Colorado where thousands of Anasazi ruins are preserved.

metate—a flat stone slab against which corn was ground.

Modified Basket Maker period—the span of Anasazi culture from A.D. 550–750.

Navajo—a present-day native American culture; the Navajo arrived in the four corners area about A.D. 1400.

nomad—a person who has no permanent home.

Nordenskiold, Gustaf—a Swede who conducted the first systematic investigation of Mesa Verde.

palynology—the study of plant pollen.

pithouse—a wood and mud Anasazi dwelling that was built around a shallow pit.

pueblo—a Spanish word meaning "village" that refers to the style of native American architecture in which small houses are clustered together on one site.

sandstone—a relatively soft, sedimentary rock.

shard—a piece of broken pottery.

sipapu—a hole in the floor of a kiva through which people of present-day pueblo cultures believe the spirits can enter the underworld.

stratigraphy—the dating of objects by looking at the layers of earth in which they were deposited.

Ute—a native American culture currently living in the area near Mesa Verde.

Wetherill, Richard—one of two cowboys credited with the discovery of Mesa Verde.

zoology—the study of animals.

Zuñi—a present-day pueblo culture in Arizona and New Mexico.

INDEX